C. S. Lewis

Can you imagine?

The true story of C. S. Lewis and his books

Catherine Mackenzie
Illustrated by Rita Ammassari

In the soft dark wood a small grave had been dug. The broken body of a much-loved dog was gently placed in the earth. Two young boys looked on solemnly as someone took a knife and carved the dog's name into a plank of wood – 'Jacksie'. The youngest boy brushed his hand across the well-known name and there and then made a decision.

Later that week he pointed at himself and told his mother, 'My name is Jacksie'. In honour of his favourite dog, Clive Staples Lewis changed his name. He wouldn't answer to anything else. Eventually his family persuaded him to try the name Jack instead – and it stuck.

In the soft dark wood a small grave had been dug.

JACKSIE

Picking up one book after another, Jack tried to decide what to take to boarding school. Leaving home in Northern Ireland would be hard. There was so much to leave behind.

Walking down the long corridor towards his mother's room, feeling hot and uncomfortable in his new school uniform, he opened the door and sighed. It was empty and had been for months. Jack's mother was dead.

'I want to remember her room the way it is,' Jack said, as he walked towards the wardrobe. Reaching out to touch the felt hats and fur coats his mother had worn, he tried to imagine her voice, but couldn't. 'Will I ever feel joy again? Why didn't God answer my prayers and make her better?' Jack questioned.

'Why didn't God answer my prayers and make her better?' Jack questioned.

Jack didn't like England at first. 'There are no green hills and the weather is very cold and damp,' he sighed. But he grew to like England and eventually settled down to his studies. However, after a while Jack no longer wanted to pray. 'I try and try to pray, but it's never good enough,' he complained. 'I try again and again to get it right, but it doesn't work. Prayer is too exhausting. I don't think I'll do it anymore,' Jack decided.

Jack didn't realise that it was only Jesus, God's Son, who was good enough to pray perfectly. Jack stopped believing in God, but sometimes found himself wishing that God was real. It would be a few years before Jack would realise that his wish had always been true.

Jack stopped believing in God, but sometimes found himself wishing that God was real.

'You've got into Wyvern College, Lewis, congratulations!' Jack smiled broadly at the news from his form teacher. But the new college did not bring him back to God. 'God does not exist,' he said to himself firmly. But then, why was he angry with God for not existing?

'We're at war with Germany!' a fellow student called out. It was 1914, the First World War had just begun.

In 1917, Jack volunteered to fight. Before he left for France he discovered a book by a Christian called George MacDonald. Jack read the book from cover to cover. In the trenches, he read a book by G. K. Chesterton. 'This book is really good too!' Jack thought. 'How can it be that two of my favourite writers believe in God?' he asked himself.

Jack read the book from
cover to cover.

'It's good to be back,' Jack declared as he returned to his studies at Oxford University. 'The war was a dreadful thing. So many young men have died. I'm glad it's over.' But Jack didn't realise that an even greater battle was raging. This battle was between Jack and God — and God was going to win.

First of all, Jack made a new friend who turned out to be a Christian. 'I really like Tolkien, even though he is a Christian. We have great discussions about books and writing, and about God. Tolkien thinks that I'll find whatever it is that I'm looking for if I turn to God.'

Jack made a new friend who turned out to be a Christian.

Jack wasn't sure about that. 'How can God make me happy? I don't believe he exists for a start. I'll keep trying to find what I'm looking for in books, or perhaps in beauty – yet these things have never given me complete joy before. Where have I been going wrong?' Then one day Jack realised that he had been looking for joy in the wrong place.

Jack was travelling on the top of a bus when he suddenly discovered something amazing. 'It's like there is a door in front of me,' he realised. 'I can either open it or keep it shut. I can either let God in or keep him out. I think I've been given a choice, but there is really only one choice that I can make. Open the door and let God in.'

Jack was travelling on the top of a bus when he suddenly discovered something amazing.

Slowly, but surely, Jack began to change. Walking past a melting snowman one winter, Jack realised something. 'Bit by bit that snowman is slowly melting – drip, drip, drip; trickle, trickle, trickle and he's just like me. Bit by bit I'm beginning to believe in God.'

Jack held his Christmas presents tightly as he hurried home to get in from the cold. 'I've spent years running away from God. I didn't realise that all that time God was really chasing after me.' Finally Jack gave in and admitted that God was God. He didn't really want to believe, but he knew he had to.

Finally Jack gave in and admitted that God was God.

Jack thought he should start going to church again. 'I'm not enjoying this,' Jack complained. 'I believe in God, but not in Jesus Christ, so why am I going to church?' he wondered. However, God's love is so great that he loved Jack even though Jack didn't want to believe in the love of God; the love that God showed by sending his Son, Jesus Christ, into the world to save sinners.

Then one day Jack and his brother, Warren, were driving a motorcycle to Whipsnade Zoo. That was when something happened. Jack explained to his friends one day, 'I set out not believing that Jesus was the Son of God – then when I arrived at the Zoo I did. I have been searching for joy all my life, but it was Jesus Christ I should have been looking for.'

I have been searching for joy all my life, but it was Jesus Christ I should have been looking for.

Jack and his university friends started a writing group. 'Let's decide on a name for it,' Jack said. Eventually they came up with: The Inklings.

Jack had started to write children's books based in the magical land of Narnia. Stories were filled with talking animals like the ones he had drawn as a child. It was great when the first printed copies arrived.

Warren held the first copy in his hand, 'Your book isn't just about talking animals. The lion, Aslan, is a bit like Jesus Christ isn't he?'

Jack smiled. 'I didn't plan to write a Christian story. It began when I imagined a faun carrying an umbrella and a queen on a sledge. It was only half way through the book that the lion came bounding in.'

Jack had started to write
children's books based in
the magical land of Narnia.

'Is it true that Jack is married,' one of The Inklings exclaimed.

'Yes, but it didn't take place in a church. Joy is ill with cancer. They got married in the hospital.' It was hard to imagine the pain and heartache Jack must be going through.

At first, Jack had married his American friend, Joy Gresham, to help her stay in the United Kingdom. The ceremony took place in a registry office – not a church. But when Joy fell ill, both she and Jack realised that they loved each other – so they were married properly.

After Joy died in 1960, Jack wrote another book about the sadness of death. 'Grief feels like fear,' Jack thought as he wrote. 'Why is it so hard to talk to God when I need him most?' he asked. Time passed, Jack came back to a peace with God.

When Joy fell ill, both she and Jack
realised that they loved each other.

Then three years later, Jack himself began to get sick. On the 22nd of November, 1963 he died. However, his Narnia books are still firm favourites. You've probably even seen the movies.

C. S. Lewis is remembered for taking a lion and a wardrobe and making them into a wonderful story. But it is the truth Jack believed, while driving on a motorcycle to Whipsnade Zoo, that is the most important part of his life – Jesus Christ is the Son of God.

C. S. Lewis is remembered for taking a lion and a wardrobe and making them into a wonderful story.

This book is dedicated to two storytellers — my parents, William and Carine Mackenzie. My love for Christ and my love for books are a cherished gift from God through them.

10 9 8 7 6 5 4 3 2 1
© Copyright 2013 Catherine Mackenzie
ISBN: 978-1-78191-160-0
Published by Christian Focus Publications,
Geanies House, Fearn, Tain, Ross-shire, IV20 1TW, Scotland, U.K.
www.christianfocus.com
Cover design by Daniel van Straaten
Printed in China

Other titles in this series: